SIX STEPS
$IX FIGURES

Copyright © 2008 Lauri J. Williams, OPTASIA CAREER & TRAINING SERVICES (L.L.C)
All rights reserved.

No part of this book may be used or reproduced in any manner
whatsoever without the express written permission of
Lauri Williams except in the case of brief quotations embodied
in critical articles and reviews.

ISBN: 1-4196-9525-8
ISBN-13: 9781419695254

Visit www.booksurge.com to order additional copies.

SIX STEPS
$IX FIGURES

A POWER PACKED GUIDE FOR YOUR CAREER GOALS & LIFE

LAURI J. WILLIAMS

Acknowledgements

To my family, Bishop D. Dewayne Rudd (Spiritual Father), and friends; who supported and encouraged me to write this book. I would like to thank everyone for their support.

Thank you Natisha Turner (natishadt@aol.com). Indeed your inspiration and creativity that you have shown creating the cover design is a work of art. You are indeed talented in what you do. Thank you for your creation of the book cover.

A special thanks to Steve Brawner, for your editing and help; to countless others who have helped this book come to fruition. I really enjoyed working with you from the beginning to the end. I have enjoyed your professionalism expertise.

Thanks Everybody.

ABOUT THE AUTHOR

LAURI WILLIAMS is a professional speaker, inspiring career coach, and job search trainer with an expertise in job search techniques and career planning. She is also a certified professional speaker for community, associations, and governmental organizations.

She also writes poetry ("Breath Taking", University of Maryland Asian Division, The Literary Magazine, September 1996, and "Who Do You Say I AM", The National Library of Poetry, Echoes of Yesterday, July 1994). Lauri Williams holds a Master's Degree in Human Resources Management and is CEO of OPTASIA CAREER & TRAINING SERVICES (L.L.C) presently based at Little Rock, Arkansas.

PREFACE:

From the Author to the Reader

DO YOU THINK a six figure salary is beyond your reach? It's not! This power-packed guide gives advice and practical tips that others who are just like you have used to land the job of their dreams.

You are no different than them, no matter what your background is. Success was their destiny, and it is yours. Following these principles can help you attain a rewarding career and a rewarding life. By staying committed to your dreams, and with much determination and persistence, you can take control of your career and your life. Your destiny starts with you.

INTRODUCTION

SUCCESS AWAITS YOU...

Six Steps Six *Figures* reflects the lessons I have learned leading countless career counseling sessions, small groups, and workshops to help people like you attain rewarding careers and reach their goals. So many of my clients have changed their lives by applying these steps that I decided I must share them with everyone.

> *After completing college, I was uncertain as to how to embark upon a career in the medical profession, but destiny pointed me in the right direction. I was referred to attend Lauri Williams' professional career counseling service. I am glad I did. I took Ms. Williams' advice and applied the key steps she talked about in her counseling. In brief, I secured a well-paying job in the medical profession.*
>
> — A.C. Porter
> Georgia

> Thanks, Lauri Williams, for your dedication and helpful insight. The superb career counseling you gave was dynamic. The key steps you taught helped me gain confidence in myself as a result of a major career transition. I was better educated about the civilian job market and knowledgeable about the interview process. The results – I landed a six figure job in the career field I often dreamed about.
> I am 100 percent happy with the service you provided me, and I will refer others to you.
>
> — **R. Hussey, (Retired Army Sergeant Major)**
> **KBR Halliburton, Iraq**

Hi Ms. Williams,

> I just wanted to send along the good news: The wonderful résumé that you created for me got me a great job with a major Contracting Corporation. After retiring from the military, I did not know what was next, but you assured me everything would be fine. Guess what! You were right again. I love my new career, and I am making 100K๏. Thanks for everything.
>
> — **T.J.W.**
> **Texas**

It is not a mere coincidence that you were drawn to this book. It is your purpose to succeed, and when you consistently apply these steps to your life, you will. I am rooting for you!

SUCCESS STEPS

THESE SIX STEPS will change not only the way you look at your career, but also the way you look at your life. They are simple, practical, and inspiring, and you can begin applying them immediately and effectively.

Step One in your journey to success is having a clear vision, so I show you how to set attainable goals and stay focused on your chief aim. As one proverb says, "As a man thinketh in his heart, so is he," so think about constant success, and it will drive you to achieve your goals.

Step Two is networking. We need one another if we want to succeed. As the poet John Donne said, "No man is an island." With this book, you will learn how to network – everything from remembering names to leaving lasting, positive impressions with the people you meet.

In **Step Three**, I teach you how to create a resume that effectively markets your achievements and accomplishments rather than just recite your life history. Then in **Step Four**, I show you how to make your resume stand out from the stack and get noticed by decision makers at small companies and Fortune 500 corporations.

In **Step Five**, I prepare you to succeed in your next job interview by teaching you about the various types of interviews and how to communicate to your prospective employers in each one. I also show you how to prepare before your interview so that you impress your potential employer the moment you walk in the door.

In **Step Six**, I teach you how to secure the deal. You will find templates and a sample letter to send following the interview to remind your potential employer why you are the best candidate for the job. I also show you how to assess salary offers and negotiate your best deal. And I show you how to leave your current employer on good terms.

Finally, I want to tell you that it doesn't matter where you are in life – it only matters where you are going. I have watched hundreds of my clients/friends apply these principles, and the success that was bottled up inside of them burst out like a soda pop that had been shaken before it was opened. Read these powerful steps and experience a wonderful change in your life. You are a millionaire and a world-changer one hundred times over. Believe you can achieve anything, and you will. Go ahead – fulfill your life's destiny. Every fiber of your being is yearning to carry out its divine mission on this Earth. Succeed! That is your purpose in life. I believe in you.

STEP ONE — VISION

WHAT YOU THINK IS WHAT YOU GET.

"Who looks outside, dreams; who looks inside, awakens."
— Carl Jung

ARE YOUR CAREER prospects like a disposable camera? You know the kind that you have to squint through the tiny viewfinder to see a distorted subject? That's a very limiting way to take a photograph, isn't it? You might get a good shot, but you can't see very far, and anything outside your field of vision might as well be on another planet.

Now think of a professional photographer. He has a collection of lenses that he carries in his bag, and he changes them based on the shot he wants. Some of his lenses focus far into the distance, while others enable him to photograph a tiny nearby flower in great detail. Wide angle lenses let him see – and share – the whole picture. Don't you want that kind of career? Don't you want that kind of life — the kind where you can choose the way you see your path?

You can have it today. No matter what you've done in the past, you can start to change the way you see the world right now, if you're willing to change your lens. How do you do that? How do you transform your views, possess a new level of thinking, and take action – meaning creating activity that breeds productivity?

This book is about creating better opportunities for yourself — creating a resume for your life, in other words. How do you make your life resume relevant? Create a vision for it with a clear objective, just like the one on your resume. While the objective is an important part of any effective job resume, for your life resume, it's the most important part because it defines what you want to do and be. Focus on a specific position or career that you prefer. Create a clear picture in your mind for the job you want in which you can prosper.

That kind of success requires a new level of thinking and a new perspective. If you succeed – and with this book, you will – you will be empowered to change the beliefs that are limiting you, and you will be able to create powerful new beliefs that build and uplift you, beliefs that propel you to your destiny!

> *"Your vision will become clear only when you can look into your own heart."* — Unknown

Four years ago, I went through a very emotionally and economically challenging career phase. I had been working hard for the wrong reasons, and I wasn't happy. I realized I was climbing a ladder of success that was leaning against the wrong building. Once I was able to acknowledge my feelings, I was able to set goals. Two months later, I established my own company, OPTASIA Career and Training Services. OPTASIA, by the way, is Hebrew for "vision," because I wanted to help clients see themselves achieve their desired goals in their careers and their lives. How can you start to improve your vision? Here are two simple but powerful techniques. The first is, **Change your lens.**

If you spend time looking through a distorted lens, you will see a distorted picture. For instance, speaking negatively about yourself and focusing on certain limiting beliefs will produce a habit of seeing yourself in a negative light. So don't go down that road.

Making daily affirmations is one of the first, most important steps to improving your life. Affirmations are positive, uplifting statements that you repeat about yourself, to yourself. When you repeat your affirmations, you are firmly imprinting these ideas into your subconscious mind. A good example is, "Each day I am getting better and better." Say this statement (or create your own) for five or ten minutes daily, concentrating your attention as clearly as possible upon your affirmation, much like you learned your multiplication tables as a child. Repeat your affirmation for 21 days, and you will notice your life begin to change. The philosopher René Descartes once said, "I think, therefore I am." We now know that, "What you think, you will be."

Keep a journal of this experience that includes "before" and "after" notes. The "before" notes will remind you how you felt and the things you often thought about as you embarked upon your affirmation quest. The "after" notes will show you the emotional changes that have occurred in you as you have tried the affirmation method. You also can record life-changing events that you experience as a result of these affirmations and your new attitude.

Individual results may vary. Don't be discouraged if you don't see your thought pattern change rapidly. As with a seed, it takes time to grow. Nurture your mind. Feed it positive words and thoughts, and wait on the harvest. As you practice this technique, you will notice that it will be easier and easier to do it. Consistently affirm yourself until uplifting ideas are imprinted on your mind, until thinking and speaking positively about yourself will be as much a part of your daily routine as brushing your teeth.

The second technique is, **Focus on your target.**

> "Drive thy business, or thy business will drive thee." — Benjamin Franklin

A photographer focuses on his subject through the viewfinder while ignoring the distractions beside him and behind him. In our lives, we focus – or hold thoughts in our head without attending to other matters – every day, even if we aren't aware that we are doing it. What are you focusing on? Are you focusing on your past, the events and failures that are already behind you and that you cannot change? Are you focusing on the things that are happening around you that are of little importance? Either way, you'll never take a clear picture. In fact, you'll never even notice the beautiful scene in front of you. Try focusing on the positive things you want. See yourself succeeding. Focus on your future today. Start now!

Have you ever used a camera with an auto-focus? At first when you point your camera at your subject, all you see is a big, blurry blob. Press the button halfway down, and suddenly everything comes into focus. You must do that with your life, and the way you do it is by creating an action plan that includes the following steps:

1. Research certain career fields and their industry average as it relates to salaries. (Research the stress level of those positions, too!)

2. Interview people you know who are currently working in the job field you want.

3. Develop your own position description by surfing job sites and collecting vacancy announcements. This helps you see what employers are looking for.

Building Blocks of Success

Activity Worksheet

It's never too early or too late to change your life.

By reviewing the building block activity sheet (**See Figure A**), we can aspire to greatness in whatever endeavors we choose, whether it be gaining a rewarding career or choosing to own a business. The key with this exercise is to provoke desire and inspire you to achieve your best in whatever you do. Remember, if you think you can, you can, but if you don't try, you will never know if you could.

Let's look at these columns and randomly study some famous people who have achieved fame and success in reaching their career goals:

Bill Gates surpassed the millionaire status in the second column (ages 16–30). In fact, he made his billions in the second column. He was a college dropout with a vision and determination. You too can succeed with the right mindset and willingness.

Oprah Winfrey made her first millions in the mid-1980s in the third column (ages 31–45). Billionaire and philanthropist Warren Buffet can be placed in this column as well.

Harland Sanders, also known as Colonel Sanders, made his millions in column five (ages 61–75) from 600 franchised Kentucky

Fried Chicken outlets. In 1960, he sold his interest in the company for $2 million to a group of investors.

See if you can place any famous or wealthy people that you know in these columns. The concept is not to get depressed if you feel life is slipping by, but to mark your progress and set your course. Your success is dependent upon your will, not your age, but there is no better time to get started than today.

OPTASIA never would have been successful had I approached it with cold, unfeeling logic. I had to believe in what I was doing just like Bill Gates, Oprah Winfrey, Warren Buffet, and Col. Sanders believed in what they were doing. Set your goals and achieve them by becoming passionate about them. Involve your emotions and all of your senses as you envision your goals, and you create life for those goals. Make success so real that you can touch it, smell it, and taste it, and you'll get there faster.

BUILDING BLOCKS OF SUCCESS

ACTIVITY WORKSHEET

FIGURE 1-A

Column1	Column 2	Column 3	Column 4	Column 5	Column 6
Ages 1-15	Ages 16-30	Ages 31-45	Ages 46-60	Ages 61-75	Ages 76-90
1	16	31	46	61	76
2	17	32	47	62	77
3	18	33	48	63	78
4	19	34	49	64	79
5	20	35	50	65	80
6	21	36	51	66	81
7	22	37	52	67	82
8	23	38	53	68	83
9	24	39	54	69	84
10	25	40	55	70	85
11	26	41	56	71	86
12	27	42	57	72	87
13	28	43	58	73	88
14	29	44	59	74	89
15	30	45	60	75	90

WHO IS RESPONSIBLE FOR Y.O.U.?

EVERY DAY OFFERS an opportunity for improvement, but only you are responsible for your personal development. Self improvement begins with you, so pursue every moment to advance your pursuit of your goals. To learn this concept, I suggest one of your daily affirmations could be, "Each day I am getting better and better."

GOAL-SETTING

IMAGINE PLANNING A trip without a destination in mind. You wash and gas up the car, pack your bags, fasten your seat belts, and turn on the ignition. Before shifting out of park, you stomp on the gas a couple of times just to hear the satisfying roar of the engine. And then ... you just stare out the windshield at the garage wall without a clue what to do next. Why? Because you never had a destination in mind; you never had a goal.

Life is like that, and your job search is like that. If you don't know where you want to go, you'll never go anywhere. Where do you want to go? Only you can answer that question.

Now imagine a trip with a destination. You know where you are going; you have set a goal. And you have that same car, all gassed up and washed and ready to go. But then you start to question: Will my car really make it that far? What if I get carsick on the way? What if my gas gauge is lying to me? Maybe I'd be better off just sitting here in the driveway.

It's one thing to know where you want to go. It's another to believe that you can actually get there. To set goals, you must begin by inspecting your mind to see what viewpoints and thought processes prevent you from having the job of your dreams or the success in life that you desire. If you find areas that inhibit you, then you must make a plan of action and transform them.

Before you begin your job search, establish clear goals that define your objectives and express what you want to accomplish. Ask yourself the following questions:

1. What can I do this year to prepare myself for finding the right job?

2. What additional knowledge or skill would I like to have to make myself more marketable?

3. What do I need to possess in order to achieve my job search goal; how can others (i.e. family, friends, and colleagues) help me?

4. How can I maximize my employer search to target the right company for me?

TIPS FOR SETTING YOUR JOB SEARCH GOALS:

1. Write S.M.A.R.T goals on paper.

2. Make sure those goals are clear and specific, not vague generalities.
   A. If you have several goals, prioritize them.
   B. Include dates and timeframes.

3. Make positive statements.

Specific = _____ YOU MUST ANSWER SIX "W" QUESTIONS (What, When, Where, Why, Who, and How)

Measurable = _____

Attainable = _____

Realistic = _____

Timely = _____

Use the sample goal form (**See Figure B**) to help you define and then achieve each of your goals. Make copies, and use one page for each goal.

SAMPLE GOAL FORM

(FIGURE 1-B)

Write down one or two goals you would like to achieve in the next week or month. Be specific.

___

List two actions you will take to obtain these goals. Be specific as possible. Also, you must include a time frame.

___

Pinpoint possible barriers to obtaining this goal. Be specific.

___

Describe action (s) you will take to overcome this barrier. Be specific.

___

Evaluate your success in obtaining this goal.

___

JOB SEARCH PLANNING CHECKLISTS

JOB SEARCHING REQUIRES effective planning. Major companies are hiring every day, but you must have a clear vision and an effective plan of action to attain the job or career of your dreams. You must decide today that you will no longer let opportunity slip by you. Make a commitment to yourself to plan ahead and be available when your time comes.

Here are three planning tools that can help bring to the surface the subtle questions or concerns associated with planning your job search.

SELF ASSESSMENT CHECKLIST

- I have two or three firm choices of careers I plan to pursue.
- I have created a list of jobs I am interested in pursuing.
- I have identified personal strengths, skills, and interests.

KNOW WHERE I WANT TO WORK CHECKLIST

- I have researched organizations or companies that might hire someone with my skills, interests, and background.
- I have identified geographic areas where I would be willing to relocate.
- I have identified 5 potential employers with whom I want to work.

- I have researched career field-entry level jobs with salaries and best geographic locations.

I AM READY AND AVAILABLE CHECKLIST

- I have an appropriate wardrobe for the interview.
- I have practiced and honed my interviewing skills.
- I have a professional-sounding answering device in case an employer calls.
- I have three professional individuals who will serve as references.
- I have prepared a portfolio to highlight my experience, skills, and talents.

JOB SEARCH PLANNING CHECKLIST

SELF-ASSESSMENT

- Career plans
- Job interests
- Personal skills and strengths

KNOW WHERE I WANT TO WORK

- Companies and compatibility factors
- Relocation issues
- Inventory file on employers
- Career fields and salary factors

I AM READY AND AVAILABLE

- Appropriate attire for interviews
- Interview skills
- Professional point of contact
- References
- Prepared Portfolio

STEP TWO

NETWORKING - INSIDER TIPS

"It's not just what you know or who you know, but it's who knows what you know."
— Author unknown

FINDING THE IDEAL job or career can seem frustrating and a bit overwhelming. That's why you can't do it alone. Thankfully, you don't have to.

Unless you live on a deserted island, you are part of your own personal network. A network is an interconnected group of people or things, so your network is you and your connections to other people, and it is the key to your success in your life. The members of your network possess a wealth of information – more than you could ever store in your own head – and their own networks contain people who can help you achieve your dreams if you add them to your network.

How do you network? I am sure this question has danced across the stage of many minds at some point or another. The answer is, there are many ways. In fact, this book cannot contain every strategy that people use to connect to people who can play a part in fulfilling their destiny. But I can suggest three steps that will help you start. First, take inventory by determining who you already know and how they can help you. Second, learn the tricks of the trade to expand your network outside your comfort zone. And third, armed with this knowledge, put yourself in the places where you can succeed.

First, take inventory. Who do you know?

The hiring process at most companies involves extensive planning. In fact, it can be months between the time an employee announces he is leaving and the time that position is open to you, and meanwhile, employers look for their current employees to fill that job. To compete with them, you need inside information, and people you know are often the best source. Whether you're talking about homes, cars, business opportunities, or jobs, the best deals are first revealed to insiders – employees, family members, friends, professional acquaintances, and then strangers. So don't be a stranger when it comes to your career! The larger your pool of friendly contacts, the better your chances of finding a golden opportunity – your ideal job.

Thankfully, you already have a larger network than you think you do, but it helps to understand how to categorize your relationships. I've listed two types of networks: professional and personal, and of course, people can be categorized as both.

Professional networks are an advantage to you as you climb the career ladder. Members of your professional network include managers, past and present; coworkers, past and present; fellow members of professional associations; and fellow members of college alumni associations. These last two associations can be particularly helpful. If you are not a member of a professional association, join one as soon as you can. They give you a chance to know and be known by others with interests that are very similar to yours. Your membership and active participation will give you inside information, and you'll have a chance to participate in training programs that make you a marketable candidate for the job you want. Surf the web and look for websites for local professional associations in your area. A good place to start is the Encyclopedia of Associations.

Personal networks are just as important. They include family, friends, fellow civic and social club members, and fellow members of your church or house of worship. You should become involved in your community if you aren't already involved. It helps you know what is going on and helps you establish your own community network bank.

Keep in mind that establishing these networks purely for your own gain won't benefit you very much. Instead, seek to make a positive impact on others' lives, and eventually it will come back to impact you. Help others fulfill their dreams, and they'll help you fulfill yours. Plus, if you show interest in others, you'll learn about their careers and their employers, and eventually you'll be able to ask for information to help you launch the career that you want.

SECOND, KNOW THE TRICKS OF THE TRADE.

Your networking approach depends largely on your relationships with others and their relevance to you. Your strategy depends on your personality, your interests, your responsibilities, and other facets of your life. But regardless of who you are, you need a plan – a networking action plan in which you outline your networking goals and the steps you will take to reach those goals. While each person's plan is different, all include the aggressive networking method, where you strategically set a goal for the number of new network contacts you want to make each hour, day or week. To illustrate: Let's say you decide to make eight new contacts per day, which equals one contact per hour. That would be 40 new people in your network each week who can help you achieve your goals.

The key to successful networking is not simply to meet as many people as possible but to leave a lasting impression on those who can help you achieve a six figure income or some other worthy goal.

Ralph Waldo Emerson said it best when he said, **"Don't go where the path may lead. Instead, go where there is no path and leave a trail."** The people who can help you achieve your goals come across many whose path leads them into, and just as quickly out of, their daily routines; therefore, you must blaze a trail so that your impact remains in their consciousness even when you are not with them.

How do you blaze that trail? Again, it depends on you. I can teach you how to network, but I cannot teach you the best way that you network. You will have to write your own book through trial and error. You will have successes and failures; the key will be to learn the right lessons from both so that you can maximize the first and minimize the second. As the wise proverb says, "Wisdom is a principle thing and in all your getting, get an understanding." This holds true in knowing how you effectively network with people.

You should incorporate a plan for remembering key people that will propel you to your destiny. If you are equipped with knowledge as to how to do so, you have taken a major step closer to your goal. If you are not equipped with that knowledge, or if you do not apply it, your network will not help you any more than it is helping you now, and it may help you less.

Remembering those key people starts with learning their names. Nothing solidifies a new relationship like the ability to recall a person's name and use it confidently in a greeting. Meanwhile, forgetting a person's name stops a relationship dead in its tracks. Few social encounters are more awkward than when one-half of your brain is focused on a conversation with an acquaintance while the other desperately flips through your mental address book trying to remember their name. This person who could have helped you achieve your goals leaves the encounter wondering why you seemed so distracted or, worse, realizes what happened.

Two powerful yet simple strategies that many of my clients have found helpful are using acronyms and keywords. Acronyms are words formed from the first letters of other words, such as NASA, which stands for National Aeronautics and Space Administration.

Creating acronyms is a simple way to help you jog your memory. Recall back to your childhood when your teacher taught you this strategy before a big exam. What are the colors of the rainbow? Why, ROYGBIV: red, orange, yellow, green, blue, indigo and violet, of course! My children use this strategy today when studying for their tests.

You can apply this strategy in meeting people as well. Want to remember the name of Paul Arnold in public affairs? He becomes "PAPA" until you know him well enough that you don't need this memory device. If you can't create an acronym that sounds like a real word, make up a word instead. In fact, silly-sounding acronyms are often easier to remember than common ones.

The image-naming keyword method is another effective way to remember the names of new contacts. This is when you create any relationship between a person's name and their physical characteristics. For instance, say I meet a person name Gregg Washington who works at Washington Mutual Corporation. I notice he has similar features to George Washington on the dollar bill. When I hear about Washington Mutual Corporation or see a dollar bill, it will trigger me to remember Gregg Washington. This helps to keep him fresh in my mind.

You don't have to use only one strategy to help you remember names. A friend of mine recently joined a church with several hundred people, and he discovered that, after several weeks, he could remember numerous faces but no names. This frustrated him, so he stuck a sheet of paper in his Bible and made a point of asking people's names, reading name tags, and listening for names in conversations. Then he wrote their names on the sheet of paper along with a few things he had learned about them and perhaps a distinguishing feature, such as "kind-looking, balding older gentleman" or "looks sort of like Cindy." Each Sunday before church, he made a point of studying that sheet, and as it grew longer, he could greet more and more people by name.

THIRD, PUT YOURSELF IN PLACES WHERE YOU CAN SUCCEED.

Finding the right lead to a job means always being ready to look in the right places. Since you never know who you are going to meet and when you may meet them, it is important that you maintain a professional appearance and keep an inventory of business cards. Treat every contact as if it were an interview. This helps you gather information that you may need in the future.

There are certain circumstances, such as training conferences and job fairs that are tailor-made for networking. Be proactive when you attend job training seminars and conferences, because the associates you meet may have knowledge about upcoming job openings and promotions. Also, be an active participant in job fairs. These are listed in your newspaper or are often scheduled at colleges and universities. Remember, at job fairs, prospective employers are looking for you as much as you are looking for them. Learn about their mission and structure so that you can decide if you want to work for them. And to ensure success, follow the Boy Scout motto: "Be prepared." Bring an updated resume that is easy to read, one or two pages in length, and applicable to a specific two or three jobs (You might want to bring more than one type of resume, in fact). Write a script for what you want to say to employers, and practice it. When you arrive, be friendly and speak clearly.

Don't wait for people or opportunities to seek you out. Instead, pursue your own destiny by never letting a good opportunity pass you by. The world is made up of two kinds of people: possibility thinkers and impossibility thinkers. Impossibility thinkers make excuses for why they can't network. They fear rejection, or they tell themselves (and others), "I am not a brown-noser." What rubbish! No man is an island, and we need each other to help us succeed in life. Instead, be a possibility thinker. Possibility thinkers pursue opportunities to network and enjoy the fruits of their networking. They aren't afraid of rejection, because they know that "No" often simply means, "Not at this time." I try to instill in my clients that he who tooteth not his own horn, it gets not tooteth. If you are good at something, tell people. You know your talents and skills far better than anyone else does, so no one can sell your product –you–like you can.

JOHN'S NETWORKING SUCCESS

I remember listening to a person quote a passage from Max Gunther's book, "The Luck Factor." He mentioned that Gunther attested that the most lucrative job offers come from acquaintances. One of my clients, who I'll call "John," would certainly agree. He managed to land a six-figure salary by applying the networking action plan and the aggressive networking method. Here's how John tells his story. "I was working for the federal government traveling around the world, and I wanted a change. I wanted a change in work environment and an increase in my income. I started searching through want ads and various internet websites, but nothing seemed to be the right fit for me. The jobs that I did particularly like were already filled by someone else. That is when I came to OPTASIA and learned more about the benefits of networking. "I gathered the information taught and modified the networking action plan to accommodate my particular career interests. I followed the plan to purposely network with 20 people per week minimum. It seemed overwhelming at first, but when I organized the contacts daily, it was a piece of cake. That was only four new people a day. That was not hard at all because I would meet a plethora of people due to my frequent traveling.

"As I continued to employ my networking action plan, my contact list grew immensely, but I was prepared because I learned name association and other networking strategies (acronyms and keywords, etc.), which helped me to remember people I met. "Using acronyms was simple for me to memorize groups of names because I was already familiar with the concept due to working for the government, which uses this concept daily. One example: I met a professional contact named Bob Arnold from Pittsburgh, Pennsylvania (BAPP). That is just one of many networking tips that help me to organize my networking contact database without forgetting people."

When John mentioned that he had a networking database, I asked him how he distinguished his contacts. John simply said, "I have a green networking business card binder, which represents money and the people who can be influential relating to my career interests. I follow up with these contacts every 30 days just to keep my name fresh in their minds."

He also mentioned that he has a red networking business card binder for those he was not sure would benefit him professionally. He would follow up with these every 45-60 days to get to know them and to let them get to know him. It was one of these contacts that helped John land his six-figure income. That's right – his life-changing opportunity came from his red binder, not his green one. You never know who will help you achieve your goals. It pays to network.

STEP THREE

YOUR MARKETING TOOL - THE RESUME

*"You don't get paid for the hour.
You get paid for the value you bring to the hour."*
— Jim Rohn

MARKETING AND YOU

JOB SEARCHING CAN be a painless process if tackled with knowledge, confidence, and the right tools. One of the most important tools is your resume.

When you are going through your job search process, you are marketing yourself in the same way a real estate agent tries to sell a house: You are finding a need and then filling it. Your customer is your potential employer, and your products are your skills and experience. Like the advertising circulars you receive in the mail from your real estate agent, your resume is a marketing piece that advertises you and gives you a chance to close the sale in an interview.

So how do you sort through your mail? Every day when I come home, I go through the stack. Bills go in a special place to be read and dealt with all at once. Personal letters and notes are read immediately. And the advertising circulars? They had better catch my eye and fill a need, or they're getting tossed.

The human resources specialist at your prospective employer opens a lot of mail. He or she doesn't have time to carefully read each resume for each job opening, so anything that doesn't catch their eye or meet their company's need could end up eliminated from the application pile.

Figure 3-A (below) is a marketing model that illustrates how the marketing process can relate to your job search endeavors. Notice the similarities between your job search and the process that marketers use to find consumers like you.

The first step in the job search process is to find a desirable employer with a need, much like a company focuses its resources on likely buyers (the reason you see beer and pickup trucks advertised during football games instead of classical music CDs and laundry detergent). To do this, you search classifieds and the internet, contact employment agencies, and network with family, friends, and professional contacts.

You then develop a way to package your desirable product-you-by submitting your resume to employers in various industries where you are willing to work. Keep a record of the responses and continue to update your resume and skills as often as possible. You should associate this process with creating your brand image in the same way that companies want you to associate their products with certain characteristics. In other words, you must demonstrate how your skills and abilities exceed that of your competitors – those people applying for the same position that you want.

The next step in the job search marketing process is to select a distribution system. This means that you must strategically plan how to get your resume to the employer. You can choose to submit via the internet on various employers' websites, by mailing your resume, or by delivering the resume in person. Either way, you want the customer/employer to know who you are, what you have to offer, and how you can make an impact on the organization.

Figure 3-A- JOB SEARCH MARKETING MODEL (JSMM)

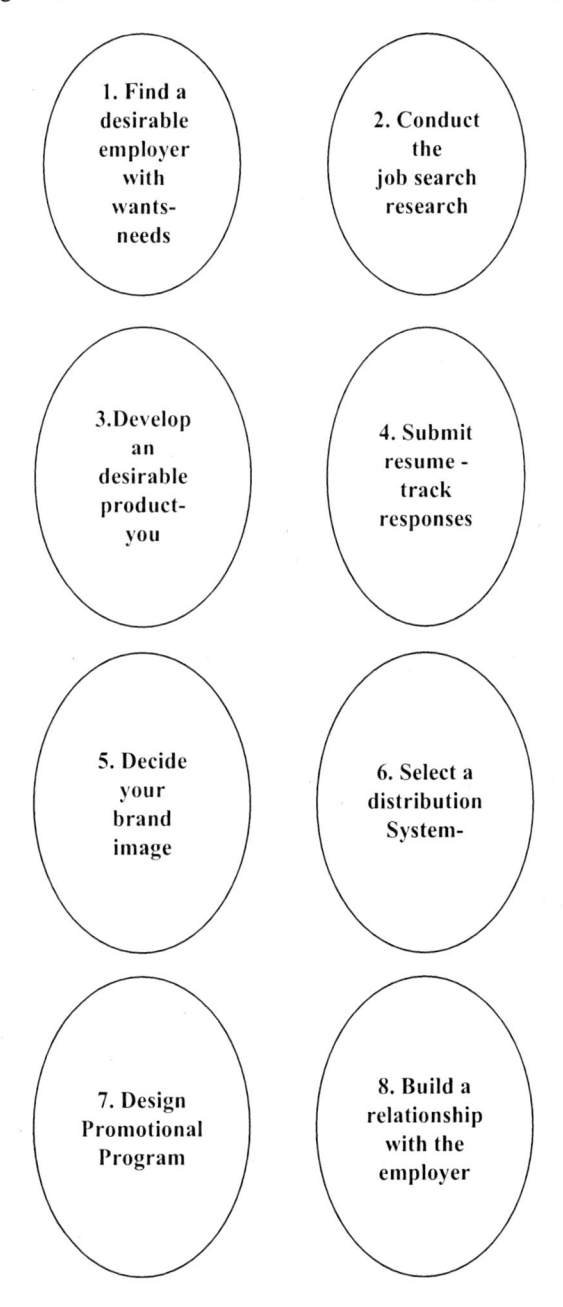

1. Find a desirable employer with wants-needs

2. Conduct the job search research

3. Develop an desirable product- you

4. Submit resume - track responses

5. Decide your brand image

6. Select a distribution System-

7. Design Promotional Program

8. Build a relationship with the employer

Designing a promotional program as it relates to selling yourself on paper is necessary in order to motivate the potential employer to contact you for an interview. This involves what advertisers call the AIDA Model. (**See Figure 3-B**). The AIDA Model consists of the four steps consumers take when making a purchase: Attention, Interest, Desire, and Action. Advertisers study how consumers take these steps to influence them to buy their products and services. Since employers go through these same steps during the hiring process, you should act like an advertiser and study them so your resume can attract their attention, pique their interest, cause them to desire your services and, finally, take action and offer you an interview and, eventually, a six figure salary. The last step in the job search marketing process consists of building a relationship with employers, continually adapting to changes in the job market in order to meet their needs.

USING YOUR RESUME EFFECTIVELY

A resume introduces you to an employer, and as previously stated, if yours isn't right, you'll be eliminated immediately. Employers do not have time to read every resume, so your goal is to get yours noticed. Two strategies that will help you do this are personifying your resume, and speaking your employer's language.

PERSONIFY YOUR RESUME

An effective resume gets the attention of employers, but a little networking beforehand can help secure your prospects of getting it into the right hands. Personifying your resume – in other words, putting a face to the page through a personal contact–may not be easy, but if you have the opportunity to establish rapport through a face-to-face meeting or a brief phone call, take every opportunity to do so. This may require a little strategic planning, but if your potential employer already knows your relevant experience when they come across your resume, they will stop and read more.

Figure B- Attention, Interest, Desire, and Action (AIDA MODEL)

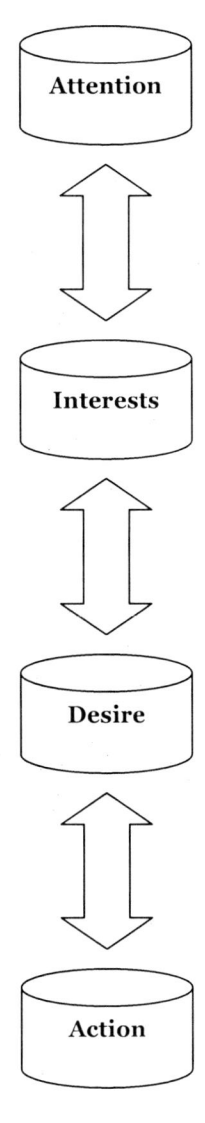

```
        Attention

           ⇕

        Interests

           ⇕

         Desire

           ⇕

         Action
```

The next time you find out about a job opening for which you are qualified, try inquiring about the hiring manager within that company. This will give you an added advantage over applicants who omit conducting this research. Remember, researching information about hiring managers and creating ways to establish rapport with them will put you ahead.

EMPLOYERS' UNIVERSAL LANGUAGE: NUMBERS

As with any consumer, employers want to know the answer to one question: "What's in it for me?" Your resume must contain impact statements or accomplishments that demonstrate how you will fulfill an employer's needs. In other words, how will you help them make a profit or accomplish their mission?

Our world is comprised of many different nationalities with many different languages, but in the corporate world, everyone understands numbers. You need to speak that language. Speaking numbers tells an employer what you did and how well you did it. In other words, numbers help make it easy to see profit. And that's what employers are looking for.

Below are a few factors employers look for when considering an applicant:

- Will the applicant help me make money?
- Will he/she help me save money?
- Does he/she manage time well?
- Has the job skill for the job?
- Is he/she a problem solver?
- Is willing to learn?
- Does he/she build relationships with internal and external customers?
- Can he/she contribute to our company's growth?
- Can he/she attract new customers?
- Can he/she help us retain existing customers?
- Is competitive (sales)

ACCOMPLISHMENTS SUPPORT THE UNIVERSAL LANGUAGE OF NUMBERS

In the upper echelon of management, especially jobs with six figure salaries, accomplishments are one of the key factors employers look for in screening applicants. When developing your resume, you must list accomplishments that demonstrate that you have completed projects that are difficult and worthwhile, and that help you stand out above your competitors. (Here's a suggestion: The next time you receive recognition or contribute significantly to your company's goals, remember to document your actions and update your resume.) Your accomplishments should be numbers-based, profit-driven, and demonstrative of corporate values. Accomplishments that are not numbers demonstrated, profit driven or demonstrate corporate value are ineffective. It can reduce your chances of getting an interview because it leaves room for questions. Keep this in mind when you draft your accomplishments-anything less can reduce your chances of getting an interview. Words and phrases that strengthen your list of accomplishments include the following: new training programs; improved, efficient operations; outstanding customer service; mission management; teamwork; emergency-planning; saved money; solved a problem.

Below are examples of less effective and more effective listings of accomplishments.

LESS EFFECTIVE:

Implemented a change over a process that improved downtime.

MORE EFFECTIVE:

Standardized an engineering change order procedures that reduced turnaround time. Improved production 27% reduced assembly-line downtime from 8 hours to 4 hours.

LESS EFFECTIVE:

Supported research and development in achieving goals for new products brought to market.

MORE EFFECTIVE:

Director of Quality Assurance R&D. Supported research and development in achieving 78 percent increase in new products brought to market.

LESS EFFECTIVE:

Improved branch ranking for sales volume to number one.

MORE EFFECTIVE:

As Senior Sales Branch Manager, improved sales production 50 percent and increased branch ranking status from number 12 to number 1 in a 14-branch district.

KEYWORD DESIGN

When you are creating your resume, make sure that it contains sufficient keywords. Keywords are words that describe your job title, skill set, knowledge base, degrees, licensures, certifications, software experience, and professional affiliations. These words are usually nouns or noun phrases; however, verbs can be used. Adding keywords increases the chance of your resume turning up on top of an employer's candidate list.

Occasionally, you will see a job announcement that includes preferred but not required specific qualification(s). This simply means that the employer would like for you to have the qualifications, but a lack of them is not a reason to screen you out. If an employer mentions that certain qualification(s) are required, then your resume must include them or it will be flagged and you will not be considered for an interview (See sample vacancy announcements).

SOME SAMPLE KEYWORDS ARE:

JOB/PROFESSION/ INDUSTRY

- Sales
- Cold-calling
- Project management
- Accounts payable

TECHNICAL TERMS

Hardware
Software

CERTIFICATIONS

- Microsoft Certification
- Six Sigma - Lean Certification
- Professional Human Resources (PHR) Certification

DEGREES

- Master's of Business Administration (MBA)
- Master's of Public Administration (MPA)
- Registered Nurse (RN)
- Bachelor of Science, Nursing (BSN)

WHERE TO FIND KEYWORDS

Keywords can be found by researching classified advertisements, newspapers, periodicals, and company websites (see sample job posting with keywords). A resource that I find helpful for accessing employer keywords is the Occupation Information Network, or O*Net, at http://online.onetcenter.org/. Try staying current with keywords. Also, maintain active involvement with your local industry's professional associations. Again, this is where networking pays off.

ELECTRONIC RESUMES

Update your electronic resume once a month to ensure that you are using current keywords. Also, change your resume to match any new jobs that you are considering applying for online. If an employer posts a position and you see that you have the right keywords, but not the mentioned qualifications, apply anyway.

HOW EMPLOYERS USE KEYWORD SEARCHES

Employers often use keywords to distinguish job candidates who have submitted resumes online. They also pay to search job board databases for candidates, conducting searches by:

- Date resume submitted;
- Past/present tense keywords;
- Location (city/town) where applicant resides;
- Most recent employer;
- Job Title;
- Salary;
- Experience Level;
- Full-time/Part-time preference;
- Company category.

Keywords help employers determine an applicant's relevancy factor – how applicable their skills are for a job opening – and reduce the number of prospects, who at that point are just names on the tops of resumes. Here's how it works.

KEYWORDS = SALES, MARKETING, ADVERTISING

Jane has the words "**sales**," "**marketing**," and "**advertising**" in her resume, and Susan only has the word "**sales**." Jane's experience is more relevant.

NOTE: Be sure not to overdo it. Resumes with too many keywords are screened out.

The relevancy factor also relates to how often candidates update their resume in an online system, so it is important that you update your electronic resume as often as possible.

Again, Jane and Susan have the same words the same number of times in their resumes, but Jane updated her resume within the last month, while Susan updated hers two months ago. Jane's resume is most recent and therefore is more relevant.

Below are sample job announcements by employers who use keywords; notice which words are repeated. Those are the words a prospective employee will need to include when she or he responds.

SAMPLE VACANCY (JOB) ANNOUNCEMENTS USING KEYWORDS

JOB ANNOUNCEMENT 1: SYSTEMS ENGINEER

The incumbent will act as main point of contact for **technical issues** at the **weapon-systems level** providing accurate and timely resolutions.

Main Duties: will include but not be limited to the following:

- Working closely with DOD customers to ensure a thorough understanding of requirements.

- Working closely with **Engineering and senior technical staff** on the production of estimations

- Engaging with customers to help plan deployment strategies and implement these converting evaluations and trials to customer wins.

- **Solve** complex scientific and engineering problems, such as the **development of new transportation systems**, the **design** of rockets, or the improvement of communications systems.

QUALIFICATIONS AND EXPERIENCE

EDUCATION/EXPERIENCE

- BSCS or equivalent, plus 4-7 years experience in middleware development, i.e. APIs, messaging software, distributed systems, or networking software
- Experience as a member of a multi-person software development team
- Must be able to work independently or on a team project

REQUIRED SKILLS:

- Experience in the deployment of network infrastructure software products
- 5+ years experience in Sales/System engineering deploying technology-focused products in the Financial Services industry
- 5+ years experience with middleware technology (TIBCO, IBM MQ, etc)
- Strong knowledge of Market Data infrastructure (Feed Handlers, FIX Engines, Pricing Engines, Ticker

Plants)
- Direct Market Data Feed connectivity (OPRA, NASDAQ, Inet, Arca, etc)
- Strong Unix/Linux skills

DESIRABLE SKILLS:

- Excellent listening skills to understand the business needs of prospects and existing customers.
- 5+ years experience in Sales/System engineering deploying technology-focused products in the Financial Services industry.
- 5+ years experience with middleware technology (TIBCO, IBM MQ, etc)
- Strong knowledge of Market Data infrastructure (Feed Handlers, FIX Engines, Pricing Engines, Ticker Plants)
- Experience developing applications in either C, C#, or JAVA
- Experience developing applications on pub/sub systems in the financial services industry Direct Market Data Feed connectivity (OPRA, NASDAQ, Inet, Arca, etc)

JOB ANNOUNCEMENT 2: MARKETING AND SALES ACCOUNT EXECUTIVE:

MAIN DUTIES:

The incumbent will be responsible for negotiating and selling online **advertising** to small to large businesses located throughout North America. Candidate must develop account opportunities, interface with editorial team to define new product offerings, work with management on sales strategy and sell/close product packages to meet their business goals.

QUALIFICATIONS AND EXPERIENCE

REQUIRED SKILLS:

- Senior Account Executive with at least 5-10 years of online **advertising sales** experience.
- Stimulates **sales** through **cold calling, telemarketing** and networking.
- Previous leadership experience required; proven negotiation skills are a must.
- Candidates should demonstrate exceptional customer focus and be confident communicators in phone, written and face-to-face settings.
- A minimum of five years proven direct sales experience primarily in advertising or Internet sales and including sales transactions with CEO/VP-level management required.
- Candidates must have excellent sales skills to successfully bring in new business and respond to an ever-changing market, and strong relationship skills for follow-up sales and service with existing accounts.
- Must be able to demonstrate strong skills in initiating high-level contacts in accounts and their agencies, acquiring sales presentation opportunities and the ability to close business.

DESIRABLE SKILLS:

- Ideal candidate has existing relationships with media buyers and advertising clients.

- An action-oriented, results-driven individual able to make sound and timely decisions in a fast-paced environment where product offerings and features change rapidly.

Resume Formats (Choosing the Right Tool)

There is no one correct way to design a resume. Choosing the right format is simply a matter of reviewing your professional experience, accomplishments, and your skills and qualifications for the position(s) you are seeking. But whatever resume format you choose, always begin with the most relevant and impressive items. After all, it's what the employer will read first. And always make sure someone you trust reads your resume to offer helpful tips. Two heads are better than one, and four eyes are better than two.

If you are transitioning or are recently discharged from the military, you will need to do a little strategic planning as it relates to your resume. A simple word of advice is this – focus on your technical and managerial competencies that are relevant to the type of civilian position you are seeking, and you will have an idea of what type of resume format to choose.

Before you decide which format you want to use, let's examine the most popular resume formats: chronological; functional; combination; targeted; and curriculum vitae. Each has pros and cons.

1. Chronological Resume Format:

A chronological resume format starts by chronologically listing your work history, with the most recent position listed first. Your academic education is listed at the end. This is particularly effective if you have consistently moved to better and better jobs, with no significant periods of unemployment. Employers typically prefer this type of resume because it's easy to see what jobs you have held and when you have held them. However, it does not always make it easier to fulfill your objective – getting the interview. Although this resume format is preferred by most selecting departments, it would be beneficial to you to research its pros and cons and conclude if it would be effective for you.

Pros:

- It is easy to read easy to highlight positions you have held.
- Shows your job stability if you have not changed jobs.
- It describes your roles and achievements.
- It reflects your increase of responsibilities and/or promotion.
- Easier to seek work similar to your current position.
- It highlights employment with impressive or important companies.

Cons:

- It calls attention to your change of company.
- It may focus too much on your age.
- It may show a lack of recycling or updated training.
- It reflects periods of inactivity or activity that is irrelevant for the position.

2. FUNCTIONAL RESUME FORMAT:

A functional resume format highlights your skills and accomplishments rather than focusing on your chronological work history. The idea is to take your achievements and skills out of the experience section and position them together at the top of the resume in a section titled "Accomplishments" or "Capabilities." This focuses the potential employer's attention on what you can do or have done rather than where or when you have worked. Only after impressing the employer with your accomplishments and skills do you present your work history as part of a brief format with dates. This format is used most often by individuals who are changing careers, have changed jobs often, or who have significant gaps in their employment history.

BELOW ARE THE PROS AND CONS:

Pros:

- It exhibits your abilities and knowledge that are most relevant to the position you want to attain.
- Because it doesn't tell your life story chronologically, it disguises periods of inactivity or successive similar jobs without promotion.
- It focuses on the fact that you have the ability to do the work even if you have no job experience actually doing it, an important point if you gained the skills serving in the military or while doing volunteer work.
- It eliminates the role repetition in similar positions.
- It helps to disguise your age, which cannot legally be a barrier to employment but often is as a practical matter. It also helps hide the fact that you have recently graduated from college or a trade school.
- It is useful in new technologies, internet, telecommunications, media, and publicity fields.

Cons:

- It does not emphasize the names of the companies for which you have worked.
- It does not stress the period of time in each position held. (This could be important with employers seeking a long-term employee.)

- It limits the description of the positions you have held and their responsibilities.

3. Combination Resume Format:

A combination resume format includes elements of the chronological and functional formats. It summarizes your skills and accomplishments first, with your employment history listed next. The combination format is more difficult to write and more complex, but it highlights your skills related to the job you are applying for and also provides the work history that employers prefer.

Pros:

- It shows very clearly that you know what you want to do and that you have the skills necessary to get the job done.
- It gives you more flexibility and creativity in describing your abilities.
- It helps to obtain a particular position.
- It eliminates information about your abilities and experience that you may prefer to exclude if you are applying for more than one position in the same company.

Cons:

- You need a different summary for each job that you choose.
- It is time-consuming.

4. Targeted Resume:

A targeted resume format is customized so that it specifically highlights the experience and skills you have that are relevant to the job you are applying for. It is similar to the combination format in that it lists skills first followed by job experience. However, while the combination format can be used for many job openings with minor changes, the targeted format is very specific to the one job you are seeking. It is more complex and labor-intensive because you must ensure that you have included as many details as possible about how your key skills relate to the job for which you are applying, but it is a popular one to use.

Keep these tips in mind when using the targeted resume format:

- Position the summary of qualifications or career highlights section at the top of your resume.
- Mirror your experience, credentials, and education to the job description; include it in the summary of qualifications section at the top of your resume.
- Last, list your experience in reverse chronological order, just like you would on a traditional resume.

Pros:

- It works well for you when you have extensive experience in your job target.
- The format provides visual breaks and is attractive to the reader.

Cons:

- It may be difficult to convey strengths in a career transition.

SAMPLE FUNCTIONAL RESUME

FRANK HOUSE
PO Box 21
Tyler, TX 55552
Telephone (555) 555-5513
Email: frank.henderson@disney.net

OBJECTIVE:

To attain marketing position that will utilize my writing skills and enable me to make a positive contribution.

Note: (Use related key words for positions you are applying for in the objective section and in the rest of the resume.)

SKILLS AND ABILITIES

WRITING SKILLS

- Produced variety of business materials, including: letters, reports, proposals and forms.
- Formulated employee policy manuals and job descriptions.
- Proof read and edited all referenced written materials.

Marketing Skills

- Designed, developed, and implemented marketing and sales campaigns, fundraisers, employee incentive programs and contests.
- Evaluated target markets and proposed marketing strategies.
- Managed all phases of direct mail projects; monitored production teams; recruited and guided vendors; oversaw print operations and coordinated mailing process.

Communication Skills

- Established and improved client communications; maintained ongoing relationships.
- Addressed customer inquiries; interpreted and delivered information; proposed suggestions; provided guidance; identified, investigated and negotiated conflicts.
- Conducted surveys and analyzed results.

Business Administrative & Management Skills

- Hired, trained, coached, supervised and evaluated staff members.
- Launched and operated sole proprietorship.
- Achieved computer proficiency; demonstrated knowledge of Microsoft Word, Excel, PowerPoint, Publisher, Adobe PhotoShop and all Internet functions.

EDUCATION AND TRAINING

Park College (University On-Line)
B.A. in English-Professional Writing

Certificate Technical Writing
Anticipated Graduation in mid 2008
Current GPA: 4.0 (on scale of 4.0)

EMPLOYMENT

01/2003 - present, Freelance Writer/Administrative
04/1999 - 07/2000, Enrollment Specialist, Sales Coordinator, Tyler, TX
08/2000 - 03/2003, Project Manager, Print & Mail Advertising, Tyler, TX
04/2003 - 12/2006, CEO & Owner, Capital Marketing Inc., Tyler, TX,

REFERENCES AVAILABLE UPON REQUEST

FUNCTIONAL RESUME FORMAT GOT JANE DOE HER IDEAL JOB

Jane, a skilled sales professional, was unsure as to which resume format to use. She discussed it with me at length and decided that the functional resume format would better fit the job she wanted. Jane said that it (functional format) better emphasized her skills and capabilities and gave her choices as to the career areas where she wanted to work. The result? She got the job.

5. CURRICULUM VITAE (CV)

A curriculum vitae (CV) is different than a resume. The word "vitae" is Latin for "life," and the curriculum vitae consists of a compilation of all the academic data and experience of a person throughout his or her life. Generally, the CV is used in Europe, Asia and Africa. The CV is accepted in American academic, science, medical, research, and technology positions. Normally it is not specific to the position for which you are applying. Its structure includes personal data, academic achievements, experience, languages, computer science, and other data, all placed in chronological order. Its layout consists of the following sections: objective; education; experience; additional information; and reference. Naturally, it is much longer than a resume.

HOW TO TURN YOUR CV INTO AN EFFECTIVE RESUME

There are important points to consider when converting your CV into an effective resume. First, you must make certain that your CV is clear, concise, complete, and up-to-date with current employment and educational information. Remember, your objective is to get the interview so you can convince the interviewer that you are the perfect candidate for the position. Second, you must show that you have the specific experience, achievements, and skills for the position you want. Also, you should omit the academic and/or work experience that is not related to the job you want, or at least summarize it in a phrase. When you successfully write your CV this way, it shows that you satisfy the characteristics required to perform the job for which you are applying.

Curriculum Vitae (CV)

Joan Van Arc
(111)222-0000
anywhereusa.com

EDUCATION

September 2007, University of Texas, Denton, TX

- Bachelor of Science in Environmental Engineering degree (EE)
- Major academic courses highlights: Company Property Management; Marketing; Economics; English
- Technology Communication; Information Management System; Modern Fabrication System

May 2006—Certified Public Accounting (CPA) Training

OCCUPATION

December 2006—present, ITT TECH investment, Dallas, TX
Application Engineer, Sales & Marketing

- Application support and industry projects tracing to sales office to achieve the sales budget and new industry market application research.

- Pay suitable visits to end users and DI for seminars and technical presentations with salesperson or distributors while collecting marketing information and competitor information analysis.

July 2005—November 2006, Intel Products Co., Dallas, TX

CPU ASSEMBLY ENGINEER

- Analyzed the yield-ratio trend, documented and solved the current problems.
- Participated in the training of marketing, business process modeling and analysis at Intel University.
- Visualized a project review with impressive presentation and multimedia animation, which was highly appreciated by department manager.

June 2003—June 2005, GE Bank Corp., LTD.
Student Intern

- Analyzed investment principles of related financial derived products.
- Formulated the scheme of market popularization and network marketing.

AWARDS, COMPETENCIES & INTERESTS

English Ability: Band 6 and the intermediate test of interpretation.

COMPUTER SKILLS:

- National Computer Level 3rd Certificate (Network Communication)
- C++, JMP, AutoCAD, 3ds Max, Photoshop

Personal Interests:

Basketball (skills); skating (speed); English (elegant); snooker (stable)

Secrets to Developing a Power-Packed Resume

You are almost ready to turn your skills and assets into a killer resume. Before you do, here are the three most important secrets that professional resume writers know are the keys to writing an effective resume.

Resume Trade Secret #1: A Concise, Precise Job Objective

The job objective quickly tells the employer (or the person reviewing the resume) whether your resume is worth reading. It must be direct and to the point because employers don't have time to read every resume from beginning to end. A weak objective, or no objective at all, means it possibly won't be read. Writing a short, precise objective makes the employer's task easier because it allows him or her to focus only on resumes from people who really want the job and whose qualifications are most relevant to the position. Remember, you must catch the eye of the employer in a few seconds.

When writing a concise job objective, consider the following tips:

- **Focus on employers' needs** – Word your objective so that it makes you sound like the person the employer is looking for. Research the company and the job announcement to find out how.

- **Avoid being vague and using clichés** – Be specific as to the job for which you are applying. Instead of saying, "obtaining an entry-level position," use the specific job title on the announcement. Also, instead of using general terms like "communication skills," use specific descriptions such as "technical writing" or "telemarketing skills." This shows that you are precise and that you know what you want.

RESUME TRADE SECRET #2: USING EFFECTIVE BRANDING STRATEGIES

Your first impression is a lasting one, so your resume and cover letter must grab the employer's attention. As with newspaper ads and magazines, **headlines are a winner**. This is an optional strategy. When used effectively, it can charm prospective employers and inspire them to read your entire resume.

SAMPLE HEADLINES:

- "Skilled Negotiator secures another multi-million dollar contract ... with ease." (You can use this headline to boast about your past sales experience).
- "Profit-Driven Executive - Strong Customer Focus"

RESUME TRADE SECRET #3: PLAYING THE NUMBERS GAME

The information in the previous sections outlined ways to speak an employer's language: numbers as they relate to profits.

There is another numbers game – the age game, and it's a game you might have to find creative ways to win if you are older or younger than the typical person who the employer expects to hire for a position. While government regulations may prohibit age discrimination, we all know it happens, and it's not hard to hide if it occurs when an employer is sifting through a stack of resumes. The goal is to get past that stage to the interview, where you can sell an employer on your qualifications and where age discrimination would be more obvious and overt.

How do you win the age game? You can do this by making your age less obvious on your resume. To illustrate, let's say that you are seeking an executive or managerial position that normally goes to people in their mid-twenties to mid-thirties, but you are in your late forties. You can delete ten years of your earliest experience to give the appearance that you are younger. Think of it this way. Employers figure most people graduate college or enter the workforce around the age of 22. Therefore, if they see 25-plus years of experience on your resume, they assume you are around the age of 47. But if they see only 10 to 12 years of experience on your resume, then they will assume that you are around the age of 32 or 34.

It works the other way, too. Suppose you have recently graduated from college, and you do not want to appear too young on your resume. In this case, you will need to gather information from your high school and college days, thus bringing your perceived age up five or 10 years. The employer will think you are at least 27 or 32 years old. How does that sound – like an interviewer calling you?

STEP FOUR

GETTING NOTICED-POSTING YOUR RESUME

"The only way to successfully manifest the life you desire ... is to keep trying until you are successful!"
— Bob Crawford

IN A COMPETITIVE market, you must develop effective strategies for gaining an advantage over your competitors – other job seekers. However, winning strategies alone won't help if you don't know where to look for the lucrative jobs.

Some job seekers are intimidated about applying for six figure jobs because they seem rare. They believe that only doctors, lawyers and CEOs make that kind of money when, in fact, many six figure jobs require skills and experience, not a graduate degree. Knowing where to find those jobs puts you ahead of the game, so turn yourself into an investigative reporter and get prepared to write your own life's story. With diligence and persistence, your work will pay off.

WHERE TO BEGIN?

Start with researching your prospective employers. For each company, ask yourself the following questions:

- What does this corporation do?
- How long has this corporation been in existence?
- Who are its competitors?
- Who are the senior staff and officers within this company?
- What are the products and/or services?
- Are there corporate/industry problems and predictions of mergers, acquisitions, pending lawsuits, and bankruptcies?
- How big is this corporation?
- How does this corporation stand out among its competitors?

Remember, it's better to learn an unpleasant answer to one of these questions before you accept a job with a company than it is to learn it afterwards.

REFERENCE RESOURCES

Where should you begin your research? The first step is to determine if a company is publicly held (traded on a stock exchange), privately owned (not listed on a stock exchange), or a subsidiary of a publicly held corporation. This will make the research process less complex. The law requires publicly held companies to report certain financial information to the Securities and Exchange Commission (SEC) and their shareholders (those who have a stake in the company). Contacting corporate officers or top management members through online and published directories is also helpful.

Another step to consider would be to contact the marketing or public relations department and request an annual report. Most public organizations produce in-house newsletters, so request copies of these as well as other published materials through their public affairs office.

Check to see if the Office of Public Liaison at any federal government agency can send you information about a public organization where you wish to work. Make sure it contains the agency's mission, history, budget, programs, and type of work. County and city governments publish handbooks and publications including extensive demographic information; check with your local government agencies or visit your library to find them. These can be useful resources for you.

PUBLISHED RESOURCES - LIBRARY

They may be old-fashioned, but libraries contain a wealth of information to help you with your job search. Each library is different, and some will be more helpful to you than others. Regional, larger public, and college libraries tend to have a large variety of business and general periodical indexes, business and technical journals, and newspapers. Many libraries have access to the internet and directories (database systems) with extensive information about major corporations (more about this later). Some may perform searches for you for free or for a small fee that will be well worth the cost. Check the nearest professional and trade associations and inquire if they have specialized libraries that you can use.

If you do not have access to a large public library or a college or university library, then your hometown library still is a great resource. At the very least, it can be an effective supplement to a tool that gets better every day– digital libraries.

DIGITAL LIBRARIES

Digital libraries, or virtual libraries, are the internet's version of the public library. Here are a few of the most useful.

- Internet Public Library (www.ipl.org)– Go to the "Reference" section and look under the "Business Directories" category. The "Business Directories" or "Employment" subcategories have links to company-related information.
- The Virtual Library (www.vlib.org)– Go to the "Business and Economics" section and look in the "Finance" category. Choose "Business Job Finder" and you will connect to the "Careers in Business" section of the site.
- Argus Clearing-House (www.argus-inc.com)– Over 400 guides are accessible through the clearinghouse. Most are HTML documents with live links, although some are only available in plain text.

There are millions of websites on the internet that contain an immeasurable amount of job information. Unfortunately, unlike the library, the information is not neatly arranged, so you will need to rely heavily on popular search tools such as Yahoo (www.yahoo.com); Google (www.google.com); Altavista (www.altavista.com) and Ask Jeeves (www.askjeeves.com). Some popular websites to find six-figure jobs are www.salary.com; www.6figurejobs.com; www.monster.com, and www.clearedconnections.com.

Whether you are looking for a job or preparing for a job interview, consider letting the internet be your guide to finding the right career for you. You can find recruiters and companies in your profession or desired profession as well as your desired geographical area. Once you find a contact for the job you're wanting, you can start to build your networking prospects (review Step 2, Networking) and create new networking channels with those recruiters and with prospective employers.

CORPORATE DIRECTORIES

Corporate directories contain valuable information about thousands of companies and are available online and in hard copy form. Hoover's publications, the Directory of Corporate Affiliations, Dunn and Bradstreet's Million Dollar Databases, and the Thomas Register are some of the most useful. Always verify the information because companies, and the names of your most important contacts, often change between updates.

Hoover's covers the world's biggest, fastest growing, and most influential enterprises through four publications: "Hoover's Handbook of American Business"; "Hoover's Handbook of Emerging Companies"; "Hoover's Handbook of World Business"; and "Hoover's Handbook of Private Companies." Its website, www.hoover's.com, provides information about 16 million companies and 600 industries, as well as the people who lead them. This database also contains a current listing of Fortune 500 companies. You'll need to pay a subscription fee to use this website from your personal computer, but your local library may have free access.

National Register Publishing (www.nationalregisterpub.com) publishes the Directory of Corporate Affiliations and is a leading provider of business reference information. It provides an in-depth view of more than 15,000 public and private businesses and their divisions, subsidiaries, and domestic and worldwide affiliates with revenues in excess of $8 million or workforces in excess of 250. It also lists non-U.S. based companies with revenues in excess of $45 million. The information also includes mergers, acquisitions, and name changes. The information is updated annually.

Likewise, Dunn and Bradstreet's Million Dollar Databases includes information on 150,000 U.S. businesses that process at least $8 million dollars in sales volume. The information is updated annually.

Thomas Publishing Company (www.thomasnet.com) produces the Thomas Register, which contains profiles of more than 100,000 U.S. companies including corporate addresses, telephone numbers, asset ratings, company executives, sales office locations, plants, and subsidiaries/division and product line information. The information is updated annually.

DIRECT RESEARCH METHOD

These days, companies prefer that you approach them directly, so it's a good idea to contact corporate officers or top management members via their website and published directories. I call this the "Direct Research Method." As you can see, this particular strategy involves going directly to a particular company's website and applying online or by mail for jobs. This is another effective way of establishing rapport before you send your resume. One thing you should keep in mind: Although you have some level of control here, you must have a clear vision as to what you want and what career interests you are pursuing because employers are not interested in playing "career matchmaker."

HOW TO USE THE DIRECT RESEARCH METHOD

Once you have found the organization(s) that interest you, investigate a little further to identify the appropriate hiring manager. This can be revealed through the company's website, other sources on the internet, directories, networking, or calling the company directly. Make sure you get the correct spelling of that person's name and his or her exact job title.

Next, write a letter with a catchy headline and a charming layout. Use a short paragraph to summarize your experience and achievements, quickly demonstrating that you have a lot to offer. Make sure that you have information about your recent position, and then sum up your letter by stating that you are interested in meeting with the person. This gives you a certain level of control: You can continue with the communication by following up, or you can let the communication die. You choose. If you are unsure as to how to use the Direct Research Method in your letter to the hiring manager(s), corporate officers, or top management members, refer back to the samples in this section.

Here's what one might look like.

Jon Doe
555 Sunny Brook Lane
Wizard Oaks, KS, 55516
(555) 121-0000
Email: **joe@yellowbrickroad.com**

WIZARD INDUSTRIES, INC.
Tin Mann Anderson
HR, Escort Dorothy
333 Toto Ave.
Bismarck, KS 55526

Dear Mr. Anderson:

Do you want to increase your company's profit margin sales in the next six months? Your competition has.

As organizations strive to improve profitability and productivity while maintaining a competitive edge, there is a growing need for senior executives who can manage change and transition while strengthening their bottom line.

I am a results-oriented leader who successfully directed telecommunications companies through a dynamic and turbulent business environment.

My accomplishments include:

> Doubled annual sales revenue;
> Developed and implemented leading-edge services;
> Devised successful marketing programs to target, penetrate, and acquire new business.

I am seeking a new challenge and am interested in relocating to the Bismarck area. I will be in Bismarck on February 1, 2008. I will call to set up an appointment.

Sincerely,

John Doe

DO'S and DON'TS in using Direct Research Method
Do's:

- Use positive statements such as "My background and experience make me a perfect fit for the job" – and then show how.
- Provide your telephone number and inform the recipient that you will follow up with a call.

Don'ts:

- Don't write statements in your letter requesting the receiver to refer you to someone in the event there is no opening; in most cases (not all), the receiver won't recommend someone they do not know.
- Never use negative statements like "I realize that I may not have the exact experience for the job." These kind of statements downplay your letter.
- Don't use statements that appear you are asking the receiver to research job openings for you. For

example, "I am requesting any possible assistance you can give concerning my pursuit of a job opening with your company."

JACK GETS THE JOB HE WANTS USING THE DIRECT RESEARCH METHOD

Jack had recently retired from the military but wanted to continue working in a job that allowed him to practice the skills he had learned in the service. He had tried to post his resume on various websites without success, so he approached me with a list of jobs he wanted to target. He wanted to know what it took to get noticed. With several counseling sessions, I learned not only what kind of job he wanted but where and for what size company.

I coached Jack on using the Direct Research Method. Two weeks later, he was singing a new song. He obtained the position he wanted with one of the companies, KBR-Halliburton, that we had targeted.

STEP FIVE

PUT YOUR BEST FOOT FORWARD- THE INTERVIEW

"Keep steadily before you the fact that all true success depends at last upon yourself."
—Theodore T. Hunger

As was stated earlier, the hiring process at most companies involves extensive planning. In fact, it can be months between the time an employee announces he is leaving and the time that position is open to you, and meanwhile, employers look for current employees who can fill that job. So when you go to your next job interview, remember that the position for which you are interviewing was planned and budgeted for well in advance.

THE INTERVIEW - WHAT IS IT?

The term "interview" can best be defined as a conversation between two or more people, interviewer and interviewee, to exchange information. Simply put, we could confine our definition to the "communication between people". However, we can say that it serves one agreeable purpose-that is to exchange needed information between all parties involved in the process.

The basic purpose or objective for an employment interview should be the attainment of desired information through effective communication. Employers set up interviews to determine if a candidate has specific qualities they are looking for to fill positions within their companies. Otherwise there would be no genuine purpose for interviewing in the first place.

There is nothing new or unusual about the process. You do it all the time in your professional and personal life. Mastering it during a job search is simply a matter of being aware of the process and tapping into your inner strength to overcome any hindrances that you may have. The more you understand, the more confident you will be. As the saying goes, a person fears what they do not understand and embraces what they can relate to.

Mastering interviewing takes great patience and much attention on the process and the people involved. Unfortunately, there is no shortcut to learning, nor does one successful interview make a person proficient.

INTERVIEW PREPARATION:

Mental conditioning is an important aspect to preparing for an interview. You must feel confident in order to convey positive impressions to the interviewer. If you do not feel confident or if you are nervous and afraid, the interviewer will know. Some interviewees might equate interviewing to confronting Goliath, but know this: Just as David prevailed, so shall you. So take the necessary steps to prepare yourself so that you will not be caught off guard, and remember to never let those Goliaths see you sweat.

"Fire" Your Fear

It's not uncommon for job seekers to become a bit fearful of interviewing, but you don't have to live with fear any more than an employer has to live with a lazy employee. How can you "fire" your fear? Some psychologists believe that facing fears is the first step in driving them away. Cognitive behavioral therapy, which focuses on changing a person's thoughts or mindset in order to change behavior, can help some people overcome depression and low self-esteem. This belief that bad thoughts lead to bad feelings is nothing new. After all, Proverbs 23:7 in the Bible states, "As a man thinketh in his heart, so is he." Employ cognitive behavioral therapy exercises and you will have less fear–you won't have to take pills to do it!

Firing Your Fear Exercise for Job-Seekers:

1. Know what you are fearful of and why.
2. Then ask basic questions, such as:

   - What will happen if I don't get the job?
   - What's the worst that can happen?
   - How will it feel to look back and laugh when I get this job?
   - How great will life look if I get this job?

3. Prioritize your fears from the least to the greatest. This will help you sort through unnecessary fears. Write down ten different circumstances and categorize them from moderate to intense.
4. Now, put yourself in each of those situations, starting with the easiest ones first. Face each item in sequence. Breathing exercises will help.

5. Record your response in a journal to help you confront a recurring fear. Later, you can evaluate and see what you did to overcome it.

Try your exercises 10 to 15 minutes a day, and you should see some noticeable results within 30 to 40 days because you have formed a habit that helps you eliminate your fears. However, keep in mind that these are suggestions – not prescribed formulas set in stone. If you feel you need additional help in this area, seek out professional counseling. You can visit the Anxiety Disorders of America website at www.adaa.org.

OTHER WAYS TO PREPARE FOR YOUR NEXT INTERVIEW

MEDITATION

Meditation means to reflect, ponder, or think over. It helps calm the mind and increases confidence in your inner self. What you pay the most attention to is what will affect your mental makeup, so meditation can be a valuable self-help tool to prepare for your next interview. When you find yourself stressed, meditate.

VISUALIZATION

Visualizing is using your imagination to picture what you want before you actually get it. Imagine yourself in an intense final interview with the officers of one of the wealthiest companies in the world, and at the end, they enthusiastically shake your hand and offer you the job. Write down how you felt while rehearsing the interview. Tackle any negative emotions so that you'll know how to confront them if they surface in the future.

You can create other visual exercises for yourself. I've been practicing one and am growing closer and closer to attaining my goal – and I'll tell you about it in my next book! Choose what works for you. If when visualizing your success you can't see mental pictures, don't worry. Sometimes acceptance from your intuitive state may come in the form of a strong feeling or a deep thought. Either way, you are planting the visualizing concept inside your super conscious mind. As you practice this method, visualizing will become easier and easier for you.

Physical Appearance and Mannerisms

Interviews can happen at any time. A chance conversation at a bank, a grocery store, or a restaurant can open the door to the job or career of your dreams. So it is up to you to invest in yourself.

Dress each day as if you are going for an interview. This will help create consistency in your life and keep you physically and mentally confident. Keep at least two perfectly clean suits or garments prepared at all times because you never know if an accident may happen with one of them. Women who are challenged financially can add a scarf or a pendant to their garment to jazz it up, while men can wear a nice tie or a collared shirt. This inexpensive gesture can make you feel better about yourself and make a lasting difference. But don't focus so much on your appearance that you detract from your communication. Your appearance and mannerisms should focus attention on what you say and do, not on what you wear.

A first impression is a lasting impression. Remember that how you look has an important bearing on how another person will respond to you. For instance, if you project that you are confident and competent, it will greatly increase your success in an interview.

Establishing trust is a critical step in this process. Focus on being natural as much as possible. Because what is natural to one person may not be to another, develop your own style and be consistent with it. People are generally quick to sense artificiality and will view you with suspicion. Practice nonverbal gestures until you feel you are communicating naturally and your movements flow smoothly.

You must maintain good eye contact! Looking away, particularly at critical moments, easily can lead a listener to believe that you don't value or believe what you have conveyed.

TRANSPORTATION:

If you do not secure reliable transportation for your interview, then you risk the chance of missing that rewarding career. Employers terminate employees for not showing up to work, so they certainly won't hire you if you miss an interview no matter what your excuse is. If you do not drive, make sure that you have arranged reliable transportation for getting back and forth to your soon-to-be job. Explore creative options and have a contingency plan if this is a problem.

TRANSPORTATION CONTINGENCY PLAN

- Public transportation (ensure it is close to work area)
- Carpooling
- Motorcycle (if you ride one)
- Bicycle (during convenient weather)
- Taxi cab (only when you really need it)
- Close friend's vehicle (make sure you pay for gas)

USING THE SWOT ANALYSIS

Preparing for the interview is a very important time. It empowers you and gives you the opportunity to take action.

But first, you need to assess yourself. One technique is a Self-SWOT Analysis, or SSWOTA. SWOT is short for Strengths, Weaknesses, Opportunities, and Threats. Businesses use the SWOT analysis to evaluate their worth and strategically plan, and you should, too, if you plan to move ahead.

Before taking the "SWOT challenge," it would help you to understand its purpose. From a business aspect, the SWOT analysis is a scan of internal and external environments. Strengths and weaknesses are internal elements, while opportunities and threats are external elements. A SWOT analysis helps companies match their resources and capabilities to that of their competitors and carve a sustainable niche in their market(s). A SSWOTA can help you uncover opportunities that you never realized existed while allowing you to eliminate and manage threats that otherwise could catch you off guard.

Preparing your SWOT Analysis

Many clients say the thought of having to prepare a SSWOTA leaves them feeling uneasy. However, they are presented with a verbal SSWOTA whenever they interview. It may appear in various forms, but it is a SSWOTA just the same. Therefore, the best way to react is to be prepared beforehand.

Remember, the basic questions involved in a Self-SWOT Analysis are:

- What are my Strengths?
- What are my Weaknesses?
- What are my Opportunities?
- What are my Threats?

You need to focus on your strengths and weaknesses because those are internal elements of which you have more control. Opportunities and threats are external elements over which you have less control. Responses should be incorporated into your SSWOTA model (see example below).

Become more familiar with the SSWOTA, and you will find that your responses in live interviews will flow smoothly and with ease. You will be able to knowledgeably describe your strengths to your prospective employer, which will give that person insight as to your suitability for the company. You also will be able to ask questions about the company that pertain to you, giving you more control over the interview process and helping decipher possible opportunities and threats. Practice pays off. Remember: The interviewer wants to see the real you.

ELEMENTS INCORPORATED IN A SSWOTA TABLE:

WHAT ARE MY STRENGTHS?

- Core competencies (i.e. expertise, abilities, proficiencies)
- Experience and education
- Personal competitive advantage amongst peers
- Financial status
- Reputation, philosophy, and values
- Strong networking (professional/personal) through which to make contacts and garner support.

What are my weaknesses? (Do you feel inexperienced, unqualified, untrained, and unskilled?)

- Lack competitive strength
- Reputation, presence, image
- Vulnerabilities: cultural, attitudinal, and behavioral
- Location, geographical (mobility)
- Gaps in mission critical skills

What are my Opportunities?

- Support system(s): family, peers, and other
- Strategic development, information, research and findings
- Technology development and innovation
- Peers/superior vulnerabilities

What are my Threats?

- Aggressive competition (other job seekers, others competing for the same business contracts)
- Personal limitations
- Corporate culture politics
- Unpredictable changes to career/business

Rules for successful Self-SWOT Analysis:

- Be truthful about your strengths and weaknesses. It's your SSWOTA.
- Make sure your SSWOTA is short and to the point. Keep it simple.

SELF-SWOT ANALYSIS

P E R S O N A L	I N T E R N A L	Your strengths	Your Weakness
S W O T	E X T E R N A L	OPPORTUNITIES	THREATS

Every area of the SWOT should be examined to achieve maximum benefit.

THE INTERVIEW IN ACTION ROLE-PLAYING EXERCISE

As in anything else, when it comes to interviewing, practice makes perfect. Mock interviews with a friend or a family member are perhaps the best way to prepare for the big day. A useful exercise is called perception checking. First, begin speaking. Talk for about three minutes or cover at least five to ten sentences about any subject you choose. When you are finished, your partner repeats back to you what he or she thought they heard you say, using phrases such as, "Let me make sure I understood you correctly. It sounded as if you said ..." The original speaker clarifies anything that was misinterpreted. After a while, reverse roles so that both parties have the same opportunity to speak – and listen. Again, if you misunderstand what the speaker is trying to say, you both work to clarify the message.

I have found this exercise to be very beneficial to me. It helps you improve your active listening skills, which involves listening to a speaker and then summarizing their key points. With consistent practice, you learn to show respect to the speaker while demonstrating that you understand what he or she is saying. It also improves your speaking skills by teaching you when you are most often misinterpreted so that you can devise more effective communication methods.

TYPES OF INTERVIEWS:

THE INFORMATIONAL INTERVIEW

Informational interviews are interviews in which you, the job seeker, initiate the meeting to exchange information and make acquaintances with a potential employer without reference to a specific job opening. It gives you the opportunity to explore career fields and learn about jobs you might pursue. This type of interview can be your key to success – unfortunately, job seekers use it far too sparingly. Treat this type of interview as if you are interviewing for a job coordinated by the hiring manager, and come prepared with thoughtful questions about the field and the company.

Samples questions for you to ask include:

- What particular experience, skills, and education are required for the job?
- What do you like or dislike about your job?
- What are the current problems or challenges facing this industry today?

Utilizing this particular type of interview gives you an advantage. You can confirm with the prospective employer if you have the required qualifications for the job you are seeking, and if not, you have the opportunity to ask for advice on how you can position yourself for future job openings (if there are none available at the moment). Before you leave the informational interview, obtain references. Ask the interviewer if he or she would be comfortable if you contact other people and use his or her name. Give that person your card, contact information, and resume. Afterwards, write a thank-you note.

Employers who like to stay acquainted with available talent, even when they do not have current job openings, are most often receptive to informational interviews. Informational interviews also work well if the employer likes sharing their knowledge or esteems the mutual friend that connected him or her with you.

ONE-ON-ONE INTERVIEW

The one-on-one interview –one interviewer with one job candidate – is the most common type. The interviewer takes one of two approaches during this type of interview: direct or indirect. The indirect style is less structured with the interviewer having some level of flexibility in the questions they ask. The direct style involves a clear agenda and a uniform set of questions asked of all candidates to make it easier to compare results. The interviewer asks specific questions about work experience, career goals, education, training, skills, or community, personal and leisure activities, so it's important to be attentive to the questions asked. Potential questions include, "What career goals have you set for yourself?" and "What experience have you had with the computer industry?" Remember to recognize the pattern the interviewer sets and follow his or her lead. Do not get frustrated and give up if you feel tense during the interview. You still have a level of control in the interview process.

Sam Peak, a client of mine, came to me for career guidance and help in preparing for his interview. Sam told me that his dream was eventually to own a landscaping business with 40 employees. I could see that his career plan was detailed, but the nagging issue (which was one of the reasons he came to see me) was that he had a limited amount of experience.

Sam did not have any apprehensions about working for someone else. In fact, he stated that he wanted to gain experience from his soon-to-be competitor so that he later could branch out on his own. Sam's dilemma was, how would he prepare for his upcoming face-to-face interview with the owner of the company?

Sam and I trained diligently, and he came out smelling like a rose. He learned a lot of lessons during his training, but he attributed his landing the job to his 30-second commercial response, a technique for responding to tough questions.

The 30-second commercial response – the equivalent of a "sound byte" in radio and television – is a statement lasting 30 seconds or less that describes your skills and professional experience that apply to the job for which you are interviewing. (You can also create them for other areas of your life.) Craft your 30-second commercial response and then practice, practice, practice to keep it precise and appealing. Thirty seconds may seem like a short amount of time, but it is long enough not only to attract your prospective employer's attention but also to persuade him or her to hire you. Talk any longer, and you risk being tuned out. A powerful 30 second commercial response can put you in the driver's seat and change the course of your career and your life.

Back to my story. When I asked Sam what question and response had gotten him the job, he said that it was when the owner asked him, "Why should I hire you to work for me?"

"I can do the job; I don't let the grass grow under my feet," he had replied. "I can eliminate your need for an extra employee. You would benefit by having a valuable employee who has experience in landscaping. I perform many duties, such as trimming and pruning hedges, trees and shrubs; planting, transplanting and maintaining flowers, plants, greenhouse and nursery stock; seeding, sodding and caring for lawns; consulting with clients on landscape designs; and plant selection and care (and more). You would gain more service requests from clients, which increases your revenue and market presence. I have a proven track record for profitable results. This can be a valuable asset to your company. I'd like to produce similar results for ABC Landscaping. I can cover ground fast, so don't delay in contacting me. I look forward to a positive response."

I train my clients to respond intellectually to their interviewer. I teach them to build rapport and to get the interviewer's attention by providing appealing responses like Sam's that leave the interviewer with something to think about. With practice, you can give a job-winning answer like Sam's.

THE PANEL INTERVIEW

The panel interview is another common interview. This is used most frequently in the public sector as well as in companies that rely heavily on team cooperation. In this type of setting, two or more interviewers question candidates in hopes of filling a job opening within their organization. Normally, the panel includes a representative from human resources, the hiring manager, and someone associated with the department that is filling the position.

The questions are typically pre-selected so that everyone is asked the same questions. When the interview process is completed, panelists rank the candidates, and the one ranking highest is offered the job.

Most job candidates find this interview style a bit frightening. Instead of focusing their attention on one interviewer, they have to face a room full of interrogators. This can be nerve-racking, especially if there is no notice given of a panel interview. But if you know how to respond, you can ace this interview and be offered the job of your dreams.

Helpful Tips for Mastering the Panel Interview

- Be prepared psychologically to expend more energy and be more alert than you would be in a one-on-one interview.
- Relax and appear calm and confident.
- Recognize the important figures or members on the panel and distinguish which role each one is fulfilling. (Try doing this when the introductions are made, remembering that the chairperson is usually the one who makes the introductions.)
- Try and identify the person for whom you soon will be working.
- Treat each person as an important individual.
- When asked a question, make eye contact with each person and speak directly to the one asking the question.
- Try and gain each person's business card before you leave the interview.
- Stay focused and adjustable.

BEHAVIORAL-BASED INTERVIEW

In behavioral-based interviews, potential employers ask specific questions about how you have performed – or behaved – in past situations in order to assess if you have the skills they are seeking. You will be asked to describe specific situations in which you were required to utilize your problem-solving, leadership, conflict resolution, or multi-tasking skills. Your responses will require not only thought but also organization as well. Be prepared to answer open-ended and closed-ended questions. An open-ended question often begins with words such as "Describe," or "When." One example would be, "Describe a time you had to respond to an irate customer." Closed-ended questions seek yes or no answers and are used mostly to verify or confirm information about the job seeker. One example would be, "You have a master's degree in human resources, correct?

Employers are looking to see if you have three types of skills: content skills, functional skills (also known as transferable skills), and adaptive skills. Content skills involve knowledge that specifically pertains to work, such as computer programming and accounting. These are expressed as nouns. Functional skills involve your relations to people, information or things and are expressed as verbs, such as organizing, managing, and communicating. Adaptive skills are personal attributes or characteristics, such as being dependable, a team player, self-directed, or punctual – adjectives, in other words.

HELPFUL TIPS FOR MASTERING THE TELEPHONE INTERVIEW:

- Examine your transferable skills and personal qualities required for the job.
- Review your resume, and mirror your responses to those qualities and skills you included in it.

- Expound on your own professional, volunteer, and educational experience in a brief illustration that emphasizes those skills and qualities.
- Use effective storytelling in your responses to draw your audience's attention.
- Make sure you respond when applicable with a PAR (Problem-Action-Result) answer. You begin by describing the problem and the action you took to solve the problem, and you end with the (positive) results of those actions. Make sure you incorporate the requirements of the position for which you are interviewing in your response to convey you are right for the job.

Telephone Interview

Many companies use telephone interviews as a way of identifying and recruiting candidates for employment, or to screen candidates to narrow the pool who will be asked to appear for a face-to-face interview. They also save the company's money when interviewing out-of-town candidates. Prepare daily for interviewing because you never know when a recruiter or a hiring person might call and ask if you have a few minutes to talk about a job. If you are prepared, you will have an advantage over your competitors before the face-to-face interviews begin.

Helpful tips for mastering the telephone interview:

- If you have a scheduled telephone interview, make sure that you will not be disturbed and that you will be accessible to your phone as scheduled.
- Find a place where you are comfortable.

- Make sure you have your resume and the questions that you have prepared to ask the interviewer are handy.
- If you have a medium-sized mirror, place it in front of you and look at it as you speak. Make sure you are smiling at all times, because it will make you sound more positive and optimistic.
- Be enthusiastic and speak professionally.
- Stand the majority of the time while you are talking. This helps your breathing intake and helps you to speak with distinction when articulating your words.
- Don't interrupt the interviewer when he or she is speaking.
- Make sure you have researched the company ahead of time; it pays to do your homework.
- If you have the opportunity, ask the interviewer about the position for which you are interviewing. This will give good information and help you develop responses.

THE DINING INTERVIEW

The purpose of the dining or luncheon interview is to assess how well you can handle yourself in a social setting. In this interview, follow the "middle ground rule." That means, order meals that are within the middle price range. Avoid wine or alcohol even if those around you are drinking. If asked, simply reply that you prefer to savor the meal and keep your mind fresh. This conveys to those around you that you value making sound decisions.

Helpful Tips for Mastering the Dining Interview:

- Let the interviewer lead. He or she is the host, and you are the guest.
- Do not sit until your host does.
- Stick to the "middle ground rule" when ordering your meal.
- Choose food that is not sticky or prone to stain.
- Do not begin eating until your interviewer eats.
- If the interviewer orders coffee and dessert, join them. It is polite; do not leave them eating alone.
- If your interviewer wants to talk business, do so. If not, wait for the right moment to interject your point.
- If you tend to get food stuck in your teeth, excuse yourself from the table for a moment to check yourself in the mirror. (You should practice this any time you are dining with others whether you are interviewing or not. It is good etiquette and it keeps you from experiencing those embarrassing moments.)
- Practice eating and conversing simultaneously.
- Thank your interviewer for the meal.

The Performance/Audition (Try-Out) Style Interview

The audition interview style is a unique process in which the interviewer takes the job-seeker through a simulation or brief exercise in order to assess their skills. This style can be used for employers that want to see the candidate in action before they make their decision, such as the military or companies looking to hire computer programmers or trainers. This style is especially beneficial to candidates, because it gives them the opportunity to demonstrate their abilities while also giving them a sense of what the job would be like if it is offered.

SAMPLE INTERVIEW QUESTIONS

No matter the style of interview, you can expect certain questions, such as these.

1. What are you looking for in a company like ours? (Here the interviewer is trying to determine if you are going to stay, or just learn the job and then leave.)
Answer: As long as there's a job to be done, I'll stay.
2. What skills can you bring to this company?
Answer: I've always been interested in this type of business. (List some facts you've learned about the company before the interview.)
3. Why did you quit your last job?
Answer: I liked it, but I feel I'll have more challenges and opportunities here.
4. What are your strengths and weaknesses? (Note: the recruiter doesn't really want to hear your weaknesses, so don't give them any.)
Answer: I am honest, reliable, and conscientious. My weakness is that I am considered by many of my friends as being too conscientious. Some say that I am a workaholic. (If you are applying for a job where you will be handling money, emphasize that you are careful and accurate. For example, mention that you like your checkbook to balance to the penny.)
5. What do you like doing in your free time? (Sports or any energetic activity are good, because they give the recruiter the idea that you are competitive.

Answer: I like reading, traveling, swimming, bowling, and tennis.

Note: Please keep in mind that these are sample questions to give you a feel for what the interviewer is looking for. You should not say anything that you can't back up.

ADDITIONAL QUESTIONS INTERVIEWERS ASK:

- Tell me about yourself.
- What activities do you enjoy the most?
- What kind of work interests you?
- Are you willing to travel?
- Are you willing to work overtime?
- What have you learned from some of the jobs or internships you have had?
- Why do you want to work here?
- What did you like/dislike about your last job?
- How long would you be willing to stay with the company?
- Tell me about your biggest accomplishments?
- How well do you work under pressure?
- What interests you most about this job?
- What can you do for us that someone else can't do?
- Tell me about a difficult problem that you have had deal with.
- Why did you leave your last job?
- What do you do when you are faced with problems or stresses at work?
- Tell me about an important goal you've set in the past and how successful you were in meeting it.
- How do you approach tasks that you dislike or that are uninteresting to you?

- Tell me about a time when you had to use verbal communication skills in order to get a point across that was important to you.
- Tell me about an experience in which you had to speak up and tell other people what you thought.
- Give me an example of a clever way you motivated your coworkers or subordinates.
- What types of decisions have you made without consulting your boss?
- Describe how you have overcome a job-related obstacle.
- Give me an example of a time when you used your fact-finding skills to gain information needed to solve a problem; then tell me how you analyzed the information and came to a decision.
- Describe the most significant written document, report, or presentation that you've completed.
- Give me an example of a time when you were able to communicate successfully with a co-worker, even when that person may not have personally liked you.
- What do you expect from a supervisor?

FOLLOW UP

Remember that your work is not done when you have finished the interview. In most cases, you can't sit back and wait for the job offer. Instead, you must follow up with your potential employer. The nice thing about follow-ups is, if they are carried out effectively, they make you appear professional and polite. Follow-ups are too important to dismiss.

Be proactive and consider follow-ups a strategic part of your job search process. They can give you the advantage you need to get the job offer over other candidates who interviewed for the position.

Use these techniques to show your continued interest in the job, but don't make it seem as though you are desperate.

There are many ways you can follow up with a prospective employer, but the most effective and lasting way is with a letter.

HELPFUL TIPS FOR WRITING THANK-YOU LETTERS:

- Always address the letter to a specific person.
- When writing a follow-up letter, be sure you have the correct titles and names of all the people who interviewed you.
- If you were interviewed by more than one person, send a separate letter or note to each person.
- Send the letter or note as soon as possible after your interview, preferably the same day but no more than 2 to 3 business days.
- Typically, you would type a letter and handwrite a note. Make sure your handwritten notes are clear and legible.
- Even if you were turned down for the job, use the thank-you letter to express your appreciation for being considered and your interest in future opportunities.
- Get in the habit of writing thank-you notes after every interview. You never know what opportunities will arise from this kind gesture.
- Alert your references ahead of time that they may be getting a phone call from your prospective employer.
- Continue your job search, even if you feel confident that you will be offered the position.
- You can follow up with a telephone call to the

employer within a week to ten days if you have not received notice the job was filled.
- Be patient. Sometimes the hiring process takes longer than the employer expects.
- Keep a good rapport with the agency you are planning to leave in case you do not get a job offer.

SAMPLE THANK-YOU LETTER

Date
Name of Address
Addressee's job title
Address
City, State, Zip code

Dear Addressee:

Thank you for the opportunity to discuss the secretarial position this morning. Our conversation gave me a better understanding of ABC Company and the requirements of the job. The additional information from Mr. Doe and John Mark was helpful in gaining a better perspective of the position.

My strong office and interpersonal skills will definitely make a contribution to your company. I am proficient in all of the computer software packages that you use and possess the customer service experience that you want.

I enjoyed meeting the office staff and touring the facility. This is clearly a quality organization with an emphasis on efficiency and a dedication to teamwork. I would consider it a privilege to join your team and look forward to hearing from you.

Again, thank you for your time and consideration.

Sincerely,
Applicant
2233 Anytime Street

Anywhere, KS 55555
(000)505-5555

SAMPLE THANK-YOU NOTE

Date
Dear Addressee,

Thank you for interviewing with me for the accountant position today. I appreciate the information that you shared with me and enjoyed meeting Ms. Smith from the Accounting Department.

My interest in working for Lund Industries is stronger than ever, and based on your description of the position, I know I can do a good job for you.

I will contact you by Tuesday of next week to learn of your decision. Again, thank you for your time and consideration.
Sincerely,
You

SAMPLE THANK-YOU NOTE

Date
Dear Addressee,

Thank you for taking the time to discuss the accounting position with me. It was a pleasure meeting you and the other panel members.

OPTASIA Industries sounds like the perfect place for me to use my skills, especially since you use the WXY system. It is the same system I have been supporting the past three years. My proven track record and accomplishments with cost-effective systems can be an asset to your company.

Again, thank you for your consideration. I look forward to hearing from you and to the possibility of joining your staff.
Sincerely,
YOU- Applicant

STEP SIX

SECURING THE DEAL- THE JOB OFFER

"What we see depends mainly on what we look for."
— John Lubbock

EVALUATING THE JOB OFFER:

You have completed the interview process, and you should commend yourself. You have followed the principles of this book and have done everything possible to impress your potential employer.

And then – success! You've been offered the job! That's even more great news to shout about. No more sweating bullets over the matter.

So, what do you do now? Do you accept the job offer? If so, do you accept the salary package as is, or do you negotiate for better terms? Indeed, these are pertinent questions that any individual should ask themselves before taking that plunge. Only you can decide what is best for you.

But at this point, when you are caught up in the excitement of getting what you wanted, it's more important than ever that you keep a level head and exercise sound judgment. Remember, your chief aim throughout this process has been to obtain the job you want with a solid company. Make sure you are equipped with all the information you need to make a decision that benefits you and your employer. To be misinformed and take a position with a company for the wrong reasons could leave you trapped in the jaws of a job that crushes your spirit, chews you to pieces, and swallows you up. On the other hand, after you have gathered your facts and counted the cost, if the scale leans heavily toward accepting the position, by all means, go for it! I am rooting for you.

Remember, this phase of the job search process is as crucial as any of the others. To be successful, you must do two things: assess the company using the information you have gathered before, during and after the interview; and assess the salary package offered to you.

ASSESSING/EVALUATING A COMPANY'S CULTURE

You should have been studying the company throughout the job search process, but the interview has given you a new perspective that will help you process the information you have learned as well as search for more. Now that you have been offered a job, it's crucial that you examine or re-examine the company's goals, strategies and plans. Ask yourself if the company has a concise mission statement that establishes objectives for management, employees, stockholders and even partners. You must be able to see eye-to-eye with the company's mission, or at least be willing to work with its plan. If you are not comfortable with what you learn, then you should be wary of accepting the offer.

Examine every aspect of the company's culture. Study the management team, which is the glue that holds everything together. Ask yourself what kind of goals management has set for the company. A company with strong management has resilience and tenacity (why, just look at Berkshire Hathaway's record). Examine the length of tenure for CEOs and other upper level management officials, which can tell you what direction the company is going and how much stability it has. For instance, General Electric's former CEO, Jack Welch, was with the company for two decades, and many proclaimed him one of the best managers of all time.

If you have not already done so, research the company to see if it is financially sound. Make sure it is not facing a major lawsuit or absorbing an astronomical debt. The last thing you need is to accept a position with a company that goes belly up. Look at its financial results – preferably each quarter to determine its stability.

Finally, there are no clear and concise guidelines set in stone as to how you assess a company's culture before accepting a job offer. Many of these aspects are intangible. Ultimately, you should work where you want to work, even if not everything on the balance sheet adds up. Regardless, the principles of this chapter should help you make your decision.

Assessing the Salary

When you are presented a job offer, make sure to let your potential employer bring up the issue of salary first. Depending on the circumstances, that salary may be negotiable, and if it is, you should give yourself an opportunity to make a good job offer even better. If the idea of negotiating makes you uncomfortable, well, think how uncomfortable you will feel learning that a co-worker hired at the same time and performing the same duties as you is making more money because he or she negotiated and you didn't. If you and the company can't come to an agreement, then you may have to ask yourself the tough question: "Do I take it, or leave it?"

As in other areas of your job search, effective negotiation begins with effective preparation. You should have a price range in mind before you walk in the door. Often, a company will mention a salary range during the interviewing process, but if it doesn't, a few hours of research could earn you thousands of dollars. Websites such as www.salary.com, www.wetfeet.com, and www.monster.com provide estimates for salaries that are appropriate for your education and skills in your geographical location. Or go to your local library and research journals and other helpful resources that can provide you with a salary range for the position you are seeking.

When you have researched your salary options and assessed your situation, you should settle on three distinct salary ranges: first, a top salary that is the best you could expect; second, a middle salary that would be a reasonable compromise and a win-win for you and your employer; and third, a bottom salary you could live with while you prove yourself to the company.

HANDLING NEGOTIATIONS

Never appear to be indecisive or nervous. You want the prospective employer to believe he or she is getting a priceless jewel– you. So stick to your guns, but be willing to compromise if need be.

FACE-TO-FACE

If you are interviewed and offered the job on the spot, you will need to be prepared to negotiate on the spot. This is why it is important to research your salary range (and the company) ahead of time. This situation can work to your advantage because it lets you know that the employer likes you, and if you play your cards right and have done your homework, then you might leave the table with the job in the bag. When faced with an on-the-spot job offer, remember three important points.

- Be a polite and thank the interviewer for the offer. Let the interviewer know you are interested in the position, even if you have changed your mind

during the interview. You never know if you will want to apply for a position with that company in the future.
- If money has been discussed (by the interviewer first), suggest a salary range. This gives you room to compromise rather than being locked into a definite amount that can cause the interviewer to withdraw the offer.
- If at some point during the discussion, you and the interviewer cannot reach an agreement, be polite and ask if you can think about the offer overnight and call the next day with your answer. Keep your word and call back promptly. It is important to notify a hiring manager of your decision about the job offer quickly, and if you wish to negotiate further issues, you should do it at once.

Responding in Writing to a Job Offer

You may want to confirm in writing about the position you were offered. Make sure that you know for certain where you will be placed. You do not want to accept the job and then find yourself in another position when you report for work.

Some companies require that you respond to their offer in writing. If so, make sure you hand-deliver it or use overnight mail. A delay can mean forfeiture of a position and will make it more difficult to apply with that company in the future. If you have concerns, be sure to express them in a clear and concise manner. This gives the hiring manager a chance to evaluate your ideas and possibly discuss them with decision makers to make a counteroffer.

Use the following guidelines for writing a negotiating letter:

- Be positive and leave room for further discussions.

- Make sure your letter is factual on all points discussed.
- Thank the organization for its interest in you, and express your interest in the organization.
- List your concerns along with suggestions, and be open to feedback.
- Convey in your letter that you are confident that a positive agreement can be reached.
- Try to compose your letter, critique it, and mail it within two to three hours of the job offer.

SAMPLE NEGOTIATION LETTER FOR JOB OFFER

7524 Anytime Manor
Cloverdale, KS 87116
(555)111-2345

Date

Company Name
Name of Person Who Offered You Job
Job Title
Address
City, State, Zip

Dear:

Thank you for offering me the position as Customer Relations Executive of the Accounting Department. I appreciate your confidence in my skills and want to assure you that I will do my best to contribute to your business objectives. I am most interested in working for your company, and I look forward to making a contribution to it.

As we discussed, based on my qualifications, work experience and market value, I am looking for a starting salary in the $35,000-$40,000 range. Can we explore the possibility of raising the salary offer to $37,500 from the initial offer of $34,000 after six months of successful performance in the position?

I am confident that we can reach a mutual agreement. If there are no objections, I will call Friday morning and schedule an appointment to discuss the issue and the criteria for a successful performance in the position.

Thank you for the job offer. I look forward to meeting with you again and starting to work soon.

Sincerely,

Jane Doe

SAMPLE JOB OFFER RESPONSE LETTER

7524 Anytime Manor
Cloverdale, KS 87116
(555)111-2345

Date

Company Name
Name of Person Who Offered You Job
Job Title
Address
City, State, Zip

Dear:

I am very pleased to accept the job offer for the position as Administration Manager. I appreciate your confidence in my skills. I am eager to join the team at (company name).

I have submitted my resignation to my employer today and, as agreed, I will be starting to work with your organization on July 8, 2007. Per your request, I have signed and enclosed the offer letter to you.

Again, thank you for providing me with this opportunity. I look forward to fulfilling your expectations.

Sincerely,

Jane Doe

CONCLUSION

SUCCESS IN LIFE depends on a simple formula: wise thoughts + wise planning = wise, informed decisions. It's true regarding your career goals and your personal life. It works whether you are negotiating a salary or finding a mate.

Every moment is a new opportunity to start making wise decisions, and every day is a chance to create a new vision for you. Accept this and you can face life optimistically, you can overcome the challenges that in the past have defeated you, and you can prepare yourself for change– because change is inevitably coming.

Remember, failure is never final. If you have missed the mark in any area of life, forgive yourself and move on. If you have recently landed a job that is less than the job of your dreams, or if you find yourself with less than the salary you deserve because you didn't know how to negotiate, don't fret! Instead, apply the six steps and prepare for a new life. It's not an accident that you received this book.

Don't simply read about the six steps. Study them and learn them so that you'll be ready for your next career move or salary negotiation. Keep this book on a special shelf – your "arsenal of knowledge shelf" – so that it will be easy to retrieve when you need it. Know that your work and preparation will pay off – if not now, then later. Success awaits you. Go forth and claim what is already yours.

I wrote this book with you in mind. I wrote it to give you that extra advantage to help you excel. Don't hesitate. Do what others who are just like you are doing. Apply this knowledge and see your destiny manifest itself. Know that I am rooting for you. You can achieve what you believe!

Special Message from the Author:

I CONSIDER IT my duty to spread the message of hope to job seekers, career professionals, and winners like you. You can prosper, you are supposed to prosper, and you will prosper if you choose to do so.

I hope that you have enjoyed this book and that you will treat its lessons as a gift to yourself. And as you climb the ladder of your God-given possibilities, I hope you will share with me the views you see. Share your success stories with me at my personal email address, LLLJ123@hotmail.com, and my company website: www.optasiatraining.com. I want to hear from you. Write me at the following address:

OPTASIA CAREER TRAINING SERVICES (L.L.C.)
P.O. Box 94797
North Little Rock, AR 72190
Phone: 1-877-771-7513

I look forward to hearing from you.